MAXIMIZE YOUR POTENTIAL

by

Rev. Michael D. Johnson

DORRANCE PUBLISHING CO
EST. 1920
PITTSBURGH, PENNSYLVANIA 15238

Dorrance Publishing Co
585 Alpha Drive
Pittsburgh, PA 15238
Visit our website at www.dorrancebookstore.com

ISBN: 979-8-8852-7174-5
eISBN: 979-8-8852-7630-6

CONTENTS

ACKNOWLEDGMENTS

1 Corinthians 15:57 (KJV): "But thanks be to God, which giveth us the victory through our Lord Jesus Christ."

This book is inspired by the late great Rev. Alfred Lee Hart, Sr. A man who taught me how to "MAXIMIZE MY POTENTIAL!" I dedicate this book to him and to one of the greatest women to have lived on this earth, my granny, Mary Primus.

A Special Thanks to the following:

- My children, Devin, Annika, and Shytirin who I am so proud of. I pray that God bless you more abundantly. I love you!

- Vicki Hart, words cannot express the love and appreciation that I have for you. You allowed me to be a part of your life for over twenty years. You will always be "Ma" to me! I am so honored and blessed to have you in my life. Thank you for the guidance, direction, advice, and motherly love that you've given to me. Love you, Ma!

- My mom, Brenda Anders, I praise God for you. I love you always.

- My sister, Carla Dewberry-Fulner, you are my girl. I love you, chick.

- Bishop Albert Carter, who I started my ministry under and raised me as one of his own. Thank you for your guidance and leadership. I love you, Pops!

- Eola Griffin, who also raised me as one of her own. You are a "Woman of Valor!" Yes, you are, Mama! I love you!

- Albert Jr, Money, Tammy, Sim, Reg, and Karen (RIH). Thanks for allowing me to be a brother to you all. I love you guys.

- Troy and Renee Tillman, you stepped in at one of the most vulnerable times in my life and took me in. I am forever grateful.

- Rev. Lawrence and Mama "J" Jackson, Thank you for allowing me to be a part of family. Love you much!

- Rev. Nyjyrus and Ciara Gurley, Nia, Tori, Jay, and, Damien, who allowed me to be a big brother. Thank you so much!

- Rev. Charles & Desha Hart, Rev. Johnny Dunomes, Rev. Lawrence Hart, the late Rev. Donald and Patricia Bell, Rev. Charlie Reed, Rev. Keith and Toya Tillman, Rev. Lonnie and Frankeya Tucker, Rev. Carlos Cage, Rev. John and Dielista Wright, Rev. Byron and Sylvia Carter, and Min. Sanovaria Govan, who have touched my life in ways you wouldn't believe. Thank you all!

- Katrina Johnson and Rhonda Richardson, thank you for helping me to grow through all the mess ups and the mistakes I have made. You have definitely helped me be the man I am today.

- To the Dewberry Family, thank you for accepting me as one of your own. I love you all! Special shout out to Grandma Bernice!!!!

- Mt. Bethel MBC, New Day MBC, Sweet Rest MBC, Greater Rock Zion MBC, Bibleway Ministries COGIC,

Sweethome MBC, First True Love World Outreach Ministries, and Growing in the Word Fellowship, who I can't call everyone by name. You have been a blessing to me, my ministry, and my family.

- A very special thanks to all of my family and friends! I love you all.

MESSAGE FROM THE AUTHOR

God has truly been good to me. Born and raised in a Louisiana country community named Woodhaven. Being raised by, Brenda Anders (mother) and Mary Primus (grandmother). Granny had me in church every time the doors opened. She didn't just have me in church, I was doing a little bit of everything. From singing to ushering to standing up giving a review in Sunday school to directing the choir to praying and reading the scripture. There wasn't nothing in the church that I didn't do. God must have allowed her to peek into my future because church is all I knew. I felt like God had something special in life for me to do. At the age of ten, God began to show visions of me standing before crowds of people.

My great-grandfather, Hollis Coney, told me that I was going to become a preacher and that God was already preparing me through the gifts I was exemplifying. I didn't understand at the time what gifts he was talking about, but I later discovered and understood the words he spoke. I began to read the bible about the Spiritual Gifts. I recognized that several of the gifts that God blessed me with were right here in scriptures. I was amazed that God would equip me with His gifts. That was just the beginning of what was to come. On August 13,1988 around 11:00 p.m., at the age of fourteen, I received and accepted my calling to preach the gospel of Jesus Christ.

Right then I realized that God had given me a great gift and with it I had a greater work to do. It wasn't until the Lord led me to a small great church in Ponchatoula, LA where I began to learn about Maximizing my Potential. It was at the Good Hope Missionary Baptist Church, under one of the greatest pastors that God has allowed me to walk with, the late great Rev. Alfred L. Hart, Sr. where I began class. If there was anyone in the world that knew how to bring out the best in me, he definitely was the one to do it. I praise and thank God for him investing in me.

Through many corrections, rebukes, and much discipline I went from just having gifts to effectively and purposely using them that God would get the glory. Pastor Hart saw the gifts/potential that I possessed and was determined to help me become the best preacher, husband, father, and man that I could be. He would always quote, "To whomever much is given, of him much is required; and to whom much was entrusted, of him more will be asked." Luke 12:48. In other words he was telling me, "With great power comes great responsibility!"

I shared this personal story with you because I truly understand that there may be someone who will read this book and know that God has something special for you to do, but you don't know what. I encourage you through prayer and faith in God that He will put you in a position that you begin Maximizing your Potential.

INTRODUCTION

Ephesians 2:10 (NLT): "For we are God's masterpiece. He has created us anew in Christ Jesus, so we can do the good things he planned for us long ago."

EVERYONE HAS A PURPOSE

One night when your mother and father got together and had sexual intercourse, nearly 100 million sperm entered into her body. As they begin their journey to the egg, many died or gave out. There were at least 200 sperm to make it to the egg, but only one entered and fertilized it, which results in pregnancy. At that point, your mother had just completed the process of getting pregnant and now the process of being pregnant begins. In the 1st trimester she experienced morning sickness, weight gain or loss, cravings or distaste of certain foods, etc. During the 2nd trimester her body was making room for the baby. So, the body aches began, stretch marks, swelling of the ankles, face, and/or fingers. But before this trimester is over, she began to feel the baby move. Finally, she's in the home stretch with the 3rd trimester. Your mother experiences some of the same discomforts as the other trimesters. In this last one, her belly button sticks out, heartburn is consistent, and shortness of breath. As the due date approaches, the baby dropped or moved lower in the abdomen, and contractions were coming more rapidly and more intense. It's time! Your mother gives birth to YOU!

Remember how it started with nearly 100 million sperm, then 200 made it to the egg, but only 1 could enter and fertilize the egg? Yes, my brother. Yes, my sister. You are the 1 who is purposed to be here.

Jeremiah 1:5 (NLT) says, "I knew you before I formed you in your mother's womb. Before you were born, I set you apart and appointed you as my prophet to the nations." Jeremiah 29:11 (NLT) says, "For I know the plans I have for you," says the Lord. "They are plans for good and not for disaster, to give you a future and a hope."

I know that there are or have been times when you ask yourself, "Why am I here? What is my purpose?" Well, you are definitely not here just to be here. God has a purpose for everyone. Now our task is to find out what it is. As a believer, if you Maximize your Potential, I believe that it will lead to you knowing your purpose.

Webster definition for maximize is "to make the most of." It says that potential refers to currently unrealized abilities with the possibility to become useful or successful. Oxford says that potential is "latent qualities or abilities that may be developed and lead to future success or usefulness." In other words, it means making the most of your qualities and abilities that may be developed and lead to success or usefulness. When you receive the gift of salvation, the holy spirit comes in and sets residence in you, bringing Spiritual gifts that are tailor made for you. Spiritual gifts are defined as a set of special abilities (potential) that God has given you to share his love and serve others. Now, as believers, we are responsible for identifying, developing, and maximizing these gifts.

HOW DO I MAXIMIZE THESE GIFTS, THESE ABILITIES, WHICH IS OUR POTENTIAL?

The purpose of this book is to answer that question. As you begin this journey in search of Maximizing Your Potential, there are some things you need and some things you need to do.

Things You Need:
1. Bible
2. A Journal

3. A Quiet Place

Things You Need to Do:
1. Pray Before and After You Read
2. Meditate Throughout the Day About What You Read
3. Spend at Least 20 Minutes a Day Intimately with God

RECOGNIZE YOUR GIFTS

WHAT ARE SPIRITUAL GIFTS?

Spiritual gifts are defined as a set of special abilities that God has given you to share his love and serve others. They are God's gifts to the church, through you. When I say, Maximize Your Potential, I am simply saying, Maximize Your Spiritual Gifts. These gifts are God's supernatural ability showing up in our lives in various ways to help fulfill the purpose he has for us.

1 Corinthians 12:4–6 (NLT) says, "There are different kinds of spiritual gifts, but the same Spirit is the source of them all. There are different kinds of service, but we serve the same Lord. God works in different ways, but it is the same God who does the work in all of us.

Let's take a look at the 3 types of Spiritual Gifts the bible gives:

1. 5-Fold Ministry Gifts

Ephesians 4:11–12 (NLT): "Now these are the gifts Christ gave to the church: the apostles, the prophets, the evangelists, the pastors, and teachers. Their responsibility is to equip God's people to do his work and build up the church, the body of Christ."

2. 9 Manifestations Gifts

1 Corinthians 12:7–11 (NLT): "A spiritual gift is given to each of us so we can help each other. To one person the Spirit gives the ability to give wise advice; to another the same Spirit gives a message of special knowledge. The same Spirit gives great faith to another, and to someone else the one Spirit gives the gift of healing. He gives one person the power to perform miracles, and another the ability to prophesy. He gives someone else the ability to discern whether a message is from the Spirit of God or from another spirit. Still another person is given the ability to speak in unknown languages, while another is given the ability to interpret what is being said. It is the one and only Spirit who distributes all these gifts. He alone decides which gift each person should have."

3. 7 Motivational Gifts

Romans 12:6–8 (NLT): "In his grace, God has given us different gifts for doing certain things well. So, if God has given you the ability to prophesy, speak out with as much faith as God has given you. If your gift is serving others, serve them well. If you are a teacher, teach well. If your gift is to encourage others, be encouraging. If it is giving, give generously. If God has given you leadership ability, take the responsibility seriously. And if you have a gift for showing kindness to others, do it gladly."

In Recognizing Your Gift, if you look at the things you do, examine why you do them, and compare them with the list of gifts, that just might be a clue to what your gift(s) is. There's no limit to how many gifts you have, but the important thing to remember is;

Luke 12:48b (NLT): When someone has been given much, much will be required in return; and when someone has been entrusted with much, even more will be required.

God not only expects us to be good stewards over our physical gifts, but most importantly, our Spiritual gifts. Remember that the Spiritual Gifts purpose is to create Christ-likeness in one another and to edify (build up), exhort (encourage), and comfort the church. In this day and time, we definitely need all the gifts in action. As you go forth in search of your gift, I pray that you would trust God and allow him to lead you.

Proverbs 3:5–6 (NLT): "Trust in the Lord with all your heart; do not depend on your own understanding. Seek his will in all you do, and he will show you which path to take."

To help you Recognize Your Gift, I have a Spiritual Gifts Survey in the rear of this book. Please take a moment before you go any further to assess yourself to identify what gifts you possess.

VISUALIZE YOUR GIFT

Once you have identified your gifts, then you will have to visualize them. In other words, you have to be able to see yourself operating in the gifts. For example, after I made it known that I had been called to preach, Pastor Albert Carter Sr. instructed me to close my eyes. Then he asked me, "Can you see yourself preaching?" My reply, "Yes sir!" He then said something that stuck with me till this day: "If you say that you have a gift and can't see yourself doing it, then that's not your gift!" Take a moment and close your eyes. Can you see yourself operating in the gifts that you have identified with in the last chapter? Before we answer that question, you need to know how to visualize your gifts.

Note: The gifts that we possess have to be developed before we can fully operate in them. But in the developing stages, we will still be able to see ourselves operating in them.

1. Know Your Gifts

To operate in the gifts that you identified with, you have to have knowledge of that gift. What it does? What it consists of? What it requires? You basically have to research and study it.

After I announced my call to preach, I asked God to give me the knowledge and wisdom, a hunger to know what it means to preach. I researched and studied the scriptures about preaching and the preachers in the bible. Then I begin to observe my pastor, other pastors, and ministers. Whatever I didn't understand or know, I asked. I wanted to know everything about preaching. After receiving knowledge of my gift, I was able to see myself working in my gift.

It is so important to know everything you can about the gifts God has freely given to you. Once you have done that, then you can visualize yourself operating in that which God has given you.

UTILIZING YOUR GIFTS

By now, I pray that you have Recognized and Visualized Your Spiritual Gifts. All the work you've done thus far would be in vain if you don't utilize it. The word utilize simply means make effective use of what you have. Let's take a closer look at using your gifts.

STIR UP YOUR GIFTS

2 Timothy 1:6a (KJV): "Wherefore I put thee in remembrance that thou stir up the gift of God, which is in thee by the laying on of my hands."

Paul was encouraging Timothy to continue to use this gift as he was charged to raise up leaders within the local churches he oversaw. Timothy had to use his spiritual gifts, keeping the fire of the empowering Holy Spirit lit within him.

There will be times when we are discouraged, tired, aggravated, and simply just don't feel like doing. I encourage you to push through the adversity and operate in your gifts. The truth of the matter is, you have no choice in the matter. God doesn't accept no excuses. You have a work to do and he has equipped you for that purpose. Whether you have realized it or not, to fully maximize your gift, that gift has to be developed. The only way it can be developed is by using it. When it comes to using your gifts there are several scriptures that I refer to:

1 Peter 4:10 (NLT): "God has given each of you a gift from his great variety of spiritual gifts. Use them well to serve one another."

Colossians 3:23 (NLT): "Work willingly at whatever you do, as though you were working for the Lord rather than for people."

Galatians 6:10 (NLT): "Therefore, whenever we have the opportunity, we should do good to everyone—especially to those in the family of faith."

It is vitally important that you understand the importance of Maximizing Your Potential, Maximizing Your Gifts. This is how you find your purpose. God uses the gifts that he gives us to accomplish his purpose in and through our lives.

Philippians 2:13 (NLT): "For God is working in you, giving you the desire and the power to do what pleases him."

The journey to Maximizing Your Potential will never end. We should always seek opportunities to use our gifts for God's glorification. It's not about us. It's all about him.

SUMMARY

I pray that you have been encouraged by this book. It was written based on my life experiences. At a very young age, I felt like a fly in a bowl of milk. I felt all alone without a purpose. Whichever way the wind blows, that's the way I went. I felt like I had no value, just worthless. But when I learned that God had a purpose for my life, that's when my journey began. Maximizing my Potential through Recognizing, Visualizing, and Utilizing my gifts helped me to understand God's purpose for my life.

Recognizing + Visualizing + Utilizing your gift(s) = your Purpose! This is an equation that can be followed throughout your lifetime. My desire is that you would Maximize your Potential in route to finding God's purpose for your life.

While on your journey, there will be sacrifices that you have to make, tests will come your way, and storms will arise. Just know that at the end of it all, your rewards will be good on earth but great in heaven.

SPIRITUAL GIFTS SURVEY

There are so many ways to be active in ministry, both in church and in the community. Should I volunteer as a Sunday School teacher? Should I join the choir or ushers? Should I be a mentor at a school or church? These are some of the questions you may ask yourself. As individuals, God made each of us unique, with particular gifts, to be powerful ministers in our own way. In this section of the book, the objective is to identify and understand the gifts God has entrusted you with.

DIRECTIONS

The Spiritual Gifts Survey will help you identify your gifts. There are no wrong answers. Rate yourself for each statement using the number that most reflects you. Try to rate yourself based on what is within you and not simply on ministry experience.

1. ____ very good at organizing and coordinating activities

2. ____ people look to you for help in figuring out right from wrong

3. ____ have a strong desire to share your faith with unbelievers

4. ____ people often come to you with their personal problems for counsel

5. ____ trust God for great things

6. ____ enjoy giving to those in serious financial need

7. ____ others know they can call upon you to assist them

8. ____ make strangers feel welcomed

9. ____ known as a scholar of the bible

10. ____ people respect you and follow your direction

11. ____ have a tender heart toward the needy and will often do what you can to help

12. ____ concerned for the spiritual welfare of other believers

13. ____ enjoy participating on service projects

14. _____   able to organize your thinking in such a way as to systematically present a bible lesson to others

15. _____   able to see how the bible relates to daily life and how to apply biblical principles to different situation

16. _____   able to delegate responsibilities to other people so as to best accomplish set goals

17. _____   able to spot a spiritual phony

18. _____   enjoy being with non-Christians because of the hope of sharing Christ with them

19. _____   enjoy encouraging those who are discouraged and down-hearted

20. _____   have a confident expectation that God will accomplish what He says

21. _____   cheerfully give well above a tithe to the work of the Lord

22. _____   feel more comfortable helping someone behind the scenes to get prepared than to do the actual teaching or leading

---

23. ____   tend to approach newcomers and visitors

24. ____   enjoy searching for answers to difficult questions in God's Word

25. ____   good at setting goals and seeing the direction a group of people should take

26. ____   enjoy visiting the sick and shut-in

27. ____   take responsibility for the spiritual growth and well-being of those under your sphere of ministry

28. ____   usually volunteer to help with tasks that need to be done

29. ____   enjoy diligent study to accurately teach the Word

30. ____   known for your insight and ability to solve problem

31. ____   good at organizing people, ideas, and resources to accomplish a specific goal

32. ____   known for good spiritual judgement

33. ____   inviting others to accept Christ as Savior

---

34. _____   often challenge others to reach their potential in Christ

35. _____   step out on faith where others will not go

36. _____   known for generosity and sacrificial giving

37. _____   eager to relieve others of tasks so they can move on to more essential areas of their ministry

38. _____   enjoy hosting guests in your home

39. _____   able to take information from several sources and come up with an answer about a subject

40. _____   able to guide and motivate people to join in the achievement of your goals

41. _____   tend to look out for those who are neglected and alienated

42. _____   willing to give of your own time to be available for the needs of others

43. _____   willing to work at a task regardless of how simple or trivial it may seem

44. _____ others comment on how much they have enjoyed, learned, or grown under your teaching

45. _____ able to offer practical solutions to difficult problems

46. _____ good at planning strategies to most effectively pursue a vision

47. _____ seek to prevent false teaching and confusion from overtaking the church

48. _____ ready and eager to tell others how to become a Christians

49. _____ available to talk to others

50. _____ see God answer prayer a lot

51. _____ often give anonymously to those in need

52. _____ enjoy helping others get their work done

53. _____ enjoy meeting new people

54. _____ take great joy in discovering bible truths

55. _____ assume leadership where there is no leader

56. ____   empathize with those who are embarrassed and humiliated and seek to comfort them

57. ____   provide long-term help for certain believers to aid them in their walk with the Lord

58. ____   feel satisfaction in seeing a job completed

59. ____   able to thoroughly study Scripture and share your findings with others

60. ____   know what to do when others around you don't know what choices to make

61. ____   often find yourself in a place of leadership

62. ____   desirous of protecting the church from error

63. ____   frequently instrumental in leading others to a saving knowledge of Jesus Christ

64. ____   encourage others to go on in the Lord

65. ____   your own faith inspires others

66. ____   willing to lower your standard of living in order to help out

---

67. ____ genuinely glad to help others

68. ____ able to extend a warmth that makes people feel at ease in strange or awkward settings

69. ____ like to study and do research

70. ____ a goal-setter

71. ____ like to spend time with those who are lonely or hurting

72. ____ desirous of protecting those in your care from evil influences and guiding them in the way of God

73. ____ very dependable for getting things done

74. ____ able to make the bible clear and relevant

75. ____ often sought out for your opinions

SCORING FOR THE SPIRITUAL GIFTS SURVEY

- Put your score on the line by the corresponding number below
- Add up the numbers across each row of answers.
- Put the total on the corresponding line for each row.

1.	16.	31.	46.	61.	A
2.	17.	32.	47.	62.	B
3.	18.	33.	48.	63.	C
4.	19.	34.	49.	64.	D
5.	20.	35.	50.	65.	E
6.	21.	36.	51.	66.	F
7.	22.	37.	52.	67.	G
8.	23.	38.	53.	68.	H
9.	24.	39.	54.	69.	I
10.	25.	40.	55.	70.	J
11.	26.	41.	56.	71.	K
12.	27.	42.	57.	72.	L
13.	28.	43.	58.	73.	M
14.	29.	44.	59.	74.	N
15.	30.	45.	60.	75.	O

- Circle the letter to the right of the lowest total. You may have more than one row totaling the same amount. Circle each of those letters.

- Match the letter(s) you have circled with the code below. Write down the name of the gift(s).

- What you wrote down, may very well be your gift(s).

GIFT LIST

A = Administration

B = Discernment

C = Evangelist

D = Exhortation

E = Faith

F = Giving

G = Helps

H = Hospitality

I = Knowledge

J = Leadership

K = Mercy

L = Pastor

M = Service

N = Teaching

O = Wisdom